The Secret of the Island

Kenneth L. Warner

The Secret of the Island

Ernst Klett Sprachen
Stuttgart

Das Hörbuch zu *The Secret of the Island* per Klett-Augmented-App

Das Hörbuch zu *The Secret of the Island* kannst du per Klett-Augmented-App herunterladen und abspielen.
Dazu installierst du die App auf dem Smartphone oder Tablet, suchst *The Secret of the Island* in der Buchliste oder über die Sucheingabe und scannst die Titelseite oder die jeweilige Kapitel-Auftaktseite, um die Audiodateien herunterzuladen.

Klett-Augmented-App kostenlos downloaden und öffnen | Bilderkennung starten und die Titelseite/Kapitel-Auftaktseite scannen | Audios laden, direkt nutzen oder speichernden und öffnen

1. Auflage 1 16 15 14 13 | 2024 23 22 21 20

Alle Drucke dieser Auflage sind unverändert und können im Unterricht nebeneinander verwendet werden.
Die letzte Zahl bezeichnet das Jahr des Druckes.

Internetadresse: www.klett-sprachen.de

Redaktion: Don Haupt
Satz: Satzkasten, Stuttgart
Umschlaggestaltung: Elmar Feuerbach
Illustrationen: Hans Köhler, Stuttgart
Umschlagbild: Alamy Images RM (Scottish Viewpoint), Abingdon, Oxon
Druck und Bindung: Medienhaus Plump GmbH, Rolandsecker Weg 33, 53619 Rheinbreitbach
Printed in Germany

ISBN 978-3-12-530901-2

9 783125 309012

Contents

Mr. Baker Mrs. Baker Jim Sally Old Martin

A Boat to the Island

Jim and Sally Baker are on holiday with their parents at Sandy Bay, a little village by the sea. They are living in a small holiday bungalow.

Jim and Sally are very happy at Sandy Bay. There are cliffs and rocks and a fine little sandy beach. About two miles from the beach there is a small island covered with bushes and trees.

Jim and Sally are good swimmers, and they spend most of their time on the beach. Sometimes an old fisherman called Martin lends them his rowing boat and they row along the cliffs and explore the caves.

One day, after lunch, Mrs. Baker says, "I can't go to the beach with you this afternoon. I have a bad headache."

1 **Jim** [dʒɪm] Abk. v. James, männl. Vorname 1 **Sally** [sæli] weibl. Vorname 1 **to be on holiday** ['hɒlədeɪ] Ferien machen 2 **by the sea** am Meer 5 **about** [ə'baut] ungfähr 7 **covered with** ['kʌvəd wɪð] bedeckt (*hier:* bewachsen) mit 8 **to spend** [spend] verbringen 9 **most of** [moʊst əv] der größte Teil 10 **fisherman** ['fɪʃəmən] Fischer 10 **called Martin** [kɔːld] mit Namen Martin 10 **to lend** [lend] leihen 11 **to row** [roʊ] rudern 11 **to explore** [ɪks'plɔː] erforschen 14 **headache** ['hedeɪk] Kopfschmerzen 14 **to have a headache** Kopfschmerzen haben

“Too much sun,” says Mr. Baker. “Lie down for an hour. Jim and Sally can go to the beach by themselves. Off you go, you two,” he says to Jim and Sally. “Here are forty pence for ice cream. Don’t be late for supper.”

On their way to the beach Jim and Sally see old Martin. He is sitting in front of his little house and smoking his pipe.
“Hallo, Martin,” says Jim. “Can we take the boat this afternoon? Mummy and Daddy are staying at home today. “
“All right,” says old Martin, “But be back by six o’clock. I need the boat this evening.”
“Thank you, Martin.” Jim and Sally go on to the beach. They find Martin’s boat and push it down to the water.

1 **to lie down** [laɪ daʊn] sich niederlegen 3 **by themselves** [ðəm'selvz] allein 3 **Off you go!** [ɒf] Fort mit euch! 4 **to be late** [leɪt] zu spät kommen 8 **to smoke** [sməʊk] rauchen 8 **pipe** [paɪp] Pfeife 12 **by six o’clock** gegen 6 Uhr 13 **evening** ['iːvnɪŋ] Abend 13 **this evening** heute Abend

"Let's row along the cliffs again and explore the caves," says Sally. "No," says Jim. "Let's do something else today. I know – let's row out to the island."
"But isn't that too far?" says Sally.
"Of course not," says Jim. "We can easily reach the island and be back by six o'clock."

They push the boat into the water and jump in. First Jim rows for a while, then Sally, but the island seems to get no nearer.
"It's farther than you think, Jim," says Sally.
"Nonsense," says Jim. "It can't be much further."
At last, after more than an hour, they reach the island. They find a small beach and pull the boat up.

4 **far** [fɑː] weit 5 **easily** *(adv.)* [ˈiːzɪli] leicht 10 **to jump** [dʒʌmp] springen 12 **to seem** [siːm] scheinen 13 **nearer** [ˈnɪərə] näher 13 **to get no nearer** nicht näher kommen 14 **farther** [ˈfɑːðə] weiter 16 **nonsense** [ˈnɒnsəns] Unsinn 21 **to pull up** [ˈpʊl ˈʌp] hinaufziehen

"Now let's go exploring," says Jim. "Come on!" The island is quite small. They can walk all round it in half an hour. Then Jim says, "Now let's go inland." He leads the way through the bushes, away from the beach.

There is no path, and it is not easy to find a way through the bushes. "We must be near the middle of the island now," says Jim.

Suddenly he stops. "Look, Sally! I can see a house." In front of them, through the bushes, they can see a small hut.

"Oh, Jim," says Sally. "Do you think that someone lives in it?"

"No, I don't think so," says Jim. "Look. There's no glass in the window, and the door is open. Let's go and see."

They go to the hut. It is quite empty. There are some old sacks in one corner and another small door at the back.

"You see?" says Jim. "There's nobody here. This is wonderful. I feel like Robinson Crusoe."

Time passes quickly on the island. At last Sally says, "Look, the sun is going down. I think we must go back soon."

1 **Come on!** ['kʌm 'ɒn] Komm (mit)! 2 **quite** *(adv.)* [kwaɪt] ganz, recht 3 **inland** ['ɪnlænd] landeinwärts 4 **to lead** [liːd] führen 4 **way** [weɪ] Weg 4 **to lead the way** vorangehen 6 **path** [pɑːθ] Pfad 7 **near** [nɪə] nahe bei, nahe an 7 **middle** [mɪdl] Mitte 14 **someone** ['sʌmwʌn] jemand 19 **open** ['oʊpən] offen 22 **empty** ['empti] leer 24 **at the back** an der Rückseite 26 **Robinson Crusoe** ['rɒbɪnsn 'kruːsəʊ] Titelgestalt eines berühmten Abenteuerromans 27 **to pass** [pɑːs] vergehen 27 **quickly** *(adv.)* ['kwɪkli] schnell 28 **to go down** [daʊn] untergehen 29 **soon** [suːn] bald

"You're right," says Jim. "We mustn't be late, or old Martin won't lend us his boat again."

They start back through the bushes towards the beach. Soon they can see the sea through the bushes. Suddenly Jim stops and catches Sally's arm.

"What's the matter, Jim?"

"The boat, Sally! Where is it?"

In front of them they can see the little beach – but it is empty. "Oh Jim, it's high tide!" says Sally. "Look – the water is much higher than before."

Together they run down the beach to the water. Far away across the sea they can see the houses and cliffs of Sandy Bay. They look on all sides, but there is no sign of the boat.

"It's gone," says Jim. "Drifted away with the tide."

They look at each other with wide eyes.

"Oh Jim!" Sally is getting rather frightened. "What can we do now?"

2 **won't = will not** [wəʊnt, wɪl nɒt] wird nicht 3 **towards** [tə'wɔːdz] auf … zu 5 **to catch** [kætʃ] ergreifen 10 **high** [haɪ] hoch 10 **tide** [taɪd] Gezeit(en) 10 **high tide** Flut 11 **higher** ['haɪə] höher 13 **across** [ə'krɒs] (quer) über 14 **side** [saɪd] Seite 15 **sign** [saɪn] Zeichen 16 **It's gone!** [ɪts gɒn] Es ist fort! 16 **to drift** [drɪft] treiben 17 **each other** [iːtʃ 'ʌðə] einander, sich 18 **frightened** ['fraɪtnd] erschreckt 18 **to get frightned** Angst bekommen

Jim and Sally are Missing

In Sandy Bay Mrs. Baker is getting rather worried.

“It’s half past seven,” she says to Mr. Baker. “Where can those two children be?”

At that moment there is a knock at the door. It is old Martin.

“Good evening, Mr. Baker,” says Martin. “Are Jim and Sally back yet? I need my boat this evening.”

He tells Mr. Baker about Jim and Sally and the boat.

Mr. Baker is rather angry. “I’m very sorry, Martin,” he says. “It’s very thoughtless of them to keep your boat so long. Let’s go down to the beach. Perhaps they are there now.”

Mr. Baker and Martin go down to the beach together, but there is no sign of Jim or Sally or Martin’s boat. It is getting dark.

Mr. Baker and Martin walk up and down the beach while they are waiting for Jim and Sally. An hour passes. Now it is quite dark. The moon is shining over the sea.

Mr. Baker is no longer angry. He is very worried.

“We must look for them, Martin,” he says. “Perhaps we can get another boat.”

“But do you know where they could be, Mr. Baker?” says Martin.

“I know that they like to row along the cliffs and explore the caves,” says Mr. Baker. “Perhaps they are stranded on the rocks somewhere. Can’t we get a boat to look for them?”

1 **worried** ['wʌrid] *hier:* besorgt, unruhig 4 **knock** [nɒk] Klopfen 7 **yet** [jet] *hier:* schon 10 **thoughtless** ['θɔːtləs] gedankenlos 10 **to keep** [kiːp] behalten 15 **dark** [dɑːk] dunkel 18 **moon** [muːn] Mond 20 **no longer** [nəʊ 'lɒŋgə] nicht mehr 23 **could** [kʊd] könnte, könntest, könnten 27 **to strand** [strænd] stranden 27 **somewhere** ['sʌmweə] irgendwo

“I think the best thing we can do, Mr. Baker,” says old Martin, “is to go to the police. They can help us.”

At the police station Mr. Ball, the policeman, listens to them with a serious face. Then he says, “This is a case for the coastguards. One moment, please.”
He picks up the telephone. “Hallo? Coastguard station, please. ...”
Mr. Baker listens anxiously while the policeman is giving his report.
“Yes ... yes ... missing since two o’clock in a small rowing boat ... two children ... One moment, please.” He looks at Mr. Baker. “How old are your children, sir?”

2 **to help** [help] helfen 4 **Ball** [bɔːl] Familienname 4 **policeman** [pəˈliːsmən] Polizist 5 **serious** [ˈsɪəriəs] ernst 6 **case** [keɪs] Fall, Angelegenheit 7 **to pick up the telephone** [ˈpɪk ʌp ðə ˈtelɪfəʊn] den Telefonhörer abnehmen 9 **anxious** [ˈæŋkʃəs] ängstlich 11 **since** [sɪns] seit

"Jim is thirteen and Sally is twelve," says Mr. Baker. "Thank you, sir." The policeman speaks into the telephone again. "Thirteen and twelve ... Yes, their father is with me now ... Right ... Right. Thank you very much."
The policeman puts the telephone down. "The coastguards have a boat with a searchlight, sir," he says to Mr. Baker. "They're on their way to the beach now and can take you with them. Please hurry."
"Thank you," says Mr. Baker, and with old Martin he runs out of the police station and down to the beach.

6 **to put down the telephone** den Telefonhörer auflegen

Night on the Island

On the island Jim and Sally are back in the little hut. They are tired and hungry and rather cold. It is dark, but the moon is shining through the window. "We must try to sleep, Sally," says Jim. "They are sure to find us tomorrow."

Jim and Sally lie down on the floor and cover themselves with the old sacks. The floor is very hard, but they are so tired that they soon fall asleep.

Suddenly Jim is wide awake. He thinks he can hear voices. He listens. No – nothing. It must be a dream. Then he hears it again – men's voices out in the bushes.

He sits up and looks out of the door of the hut. Four men are coming out of the bushes. He can see them

2 **to be cold** frieren 4 **to sleep** [sliːp] schlafen 5 **sure** [ʃʊə] sicher 4 **they are sure to find us** ['faɪnd əs] sie finden uns sicherlich 5 **tomorrow** [tə'mɒrəʊ] morgen 7 **themselves** [ðəm'selvz] sich 8 **hard** [hɑːd] hart 8 **to fall asleep** ['fɔːl əs'liːp] einschlafen 9 **wide** [waɪd] weit 9 **awake** [əw'eɪk] wach 9 **wide awake** hellwach 10 **voice** [vɔɪs] Stimme 10 **dream** [driːm] Traum 13 **to sit up** sich aufrichten

clearly in the moonlight. They are carrying heavy boxes and are coming towards the hut.

Suddenly Jim is afraid. Quickly he wakes Sally. "Quick! People are coming. Out of the back door. Quick!"

He pulls her with him through the small back door, and they crouch down behind the wall of the hut.

They hear the men come into the hut and put their boxes down on the floor. There is a murmur of voices, and then a man says, "Well, that's all. You'd better count them." Another voice says, "I hope you're not swindling me." The first voice laughs and says, "You know me, Mr. Carstairs."

Mr. Carstairs? There is a Mr. Carstairs in Sandy Bay. He lives alone in an old house in the village with a high wall around it and he has a big, dangerous dog. Nobody likes him. But what is Mr. Carstairs doing on the island in the middle of the night?

"Sally," whispers Jim, "let's crawl round to the window. I want to see what they are doing."

"Be careful, Jim," whispers Sally. "Don't let them see you."

They crawl round to the window and Jim raises himself so that he can just look in.

The four men are crouching round one of the big boxes, which is now open. One of the men is shining a torch into the box. Jim puts his hand to his mouth to stop a cry of astonishment. The box is

1 **clearly** *(adv.)* ['klɪəli] deutlich 1 **moonlight** ['muːnlaɪt] Mondschein 3 **to be afraid** [ə'freɪd] Angst haben 3 **to wake s.b.** [weɪk] jemanden aufwecken 4 **back door** ['bæk'dɔː] Hintertür 7 **to crouch** [kraʊtʃ] sich ducken 9 **murmur** ['mɜːmə] Gemurmel 11 **you'd better = you had better** [juːd 'betə] es wäre besser, wenn du … 11 **to count** [kaʊnt] zählen 12 **to swindle s.b.** ['swɪndl] jemanden beschwindeln 16 **dangerous** ['deɪndʒrəs] gefährlich 17 **nobody** ['nəʊbədi] niemand 19 **to whisper** ['wɪspə] flüstern 19 **to crawl** ['krɔːl] kriechen 21 **careful** ['kɛəfʊl] vorsichtig 24 **to raise oneself** ['reɪz wʌnself] sich aufrichten 24 **to look in** hineinschauen 27 **to shine** [ʃaɪn] leuchten, scheinen 27 **torch** [tɔːtʃ] Taschenlampe 27 **to shine a torch** mit einer Taschenlampe leuchten 28 **cry** [kraɪ] (Auf)Schrei 28 **astonishment** [əs'tɒnɪʃmənt] Erstaunen

full of gold watches, necklaces and rings, all shining and sparkling in the light.

Jim crouches down again by Sally. "Smugglers, Sally," he whispers excitedly. "Those boxes are full of jewelry. And Mr. Carstairs is there with a big diamond necklace in his hands. He's one of them."

"Let's go away, Jim," whispers Sally. "I'm so frightened. If they catch us ..."

"Wait," whispers Jim. "I have an idea." He thinks for a moment. "Listen. These people must have a boat. Perhaps we can take it while they are still in the hut. Let's go down to the beach. Hurry – there's no time to lose."

1 **gold** [gəʊld] Gold 1 **necklace** ['neklɪs] Halskette 1 **ring** [rɪŋ] (Finger)Ring 2 **to sparkle** ['spɑːkl] funkeln 2 **light** [laɪt] Licht 3 **smuggler** ['smʌglə] Schmuggler 4 **excitedly** *(adv.)* [ɪk'saɪtɪdli] aufgeregt 5 **jewelry** ['dʒuːəlri] Schmuck(waren) 6 **diamond** ['daɪəmənd] Diamant 8 **to catch** [kætʃ] fangen 9 **idea** [aɪ'diːə] Idee

The Search

The coastguard cutter is moving slowly along the coast. The officer in front is shining the searchlight along the cliffs and the rocks near the water. Mr. Baker is standing at his side.
"Jim! Sally!" Again and again Mr. Baker calls their names, but there is no answer from the dark cliffs.
At last the coastguard officer says, "We are more than five miles from Sandy Bay now, and they only have a rowing boat. They couldn't have come farther than this. I think we must go back now, sir."
"Right," says Mr. Baker. "But there are more cliffs on the other side of Sandy Bay. We must look there, too."

1 **to move** [muːv] sich bewegen, fahren 1 **slowly** *(adv.)* [ˈsləʊli] langsam 2 **officer** [ˈɒfɪsə] Offizier 5 **again and again** immer wieder 9 **they couldn't (= could not) have come …** [ðeɪ ˈkʊdnt] sie können unmöglich … gekommen sein 10 **than this** [ðæn ˈðɪs] als bis hierher

The coastguard cutter turns back towards Sandy Bay. Its searchlight is still sweeping slowly across the sea. Mr. Baker and old Martin are standing together. Their eyes are following the searchlight. Suddenly Martin shouts. “Look! Look!”
“Where? What is it, Martin?” says Mr. Baker.
“A boat! Quick! Turn the searchlight!”
“One moment,” says the coastguard officer. He turns the searchlight a little to the left.
“There! There!” shouts Martin. “And it’s my boat!”
They can all see it – a small rowing boat about half a mile away.
The motor roars, and the cutter speeds across the dark sea. Soon they reach the boat and make a terrible discovery.

2 **to sweep** [swiːp] fegen, kehren 2 **to sweep across** *hier:* hinstreichen über 13 **to roar** [rɔː] brüllen, donnern 13 **to speed** [spiːd] eilen 15 **terrible** ['terəbl] schrecklich 15 **discovery** [dɪs'kʌvəri] Entdeckung

"Empty!" Fear grips Mr. Baker's heart.

A hand touches his shoulder. "Don't worry, sir," says the coastguard officer. "The boat is in order and the oars are still in it. Perhaps they landed somewhere, and the boat drifted away with the tide. That can easily happen."

"Landed?" says Mr. Baker. "But where? Where can they be?"

For a moment nobody says a word.

Then old Martin says, "There is one possibility."

"What's that?"

"The island."

"Ah," says the coastguard officer. "Yes. You're right. That is possible."

"Then hurry!" says Mr. Baker. "Full speed for the island."

1 **fear** [fɪə] Furcht 1 **to grip** [grɪp] packen, ergreifen 1 **heart** [hɑːt] Herz 2 **to touch** [tʌtʃ] berühren 2 **shoulder** ['ʃəʊldə] Schulter 3 **order** ['ɔːdə] Ordnung 4 **to land** [lænd] landen 6 **to happen** ['hæpən] vorkommen, passieren 10 **possibility** [pɒsə'bɪləti] Möglichkeit 14 **possible** ['pɒsəbl] möglich 15 **speed** [spiːd] Geschwindigkeit 15 **full speed for ...** mit voller Geschwindigkeit nach / zur ...

Escape!

Jim and Sally are hurrying through the dark bushes towards the beach.
"Look Sally," Jim suddenly stops and takes her arm. "You see? There are two boats on the beach. Two rowing boats."
Sally looks through the bushes towards the beach. "Oh yes."
"Then come on. We can take one of the boats and be away before they know."
"But wait, Jim." Sally catches his arm.
"What's the matter, Sally? Don't be afraid."
"But look, Jim. There's a man on the beach near the boats."
Jim looks again. A man is sitting near the two boats on the beach and smoking a cigarette. They can see the red point of his cigarette.

15 **to smoke** ['sməʊk] rauchen 15 **cigarette** [sɪgə'ret] Zigarette 16 **red** [red] rot 16 **point** [pɔɪnt] Punkt

"Oh yes," says Jim. "He's guarding the boats, of course. What can we do now?"

"I don't know, Jim," says Sally. "But don't do anything silly. Perhaps he has a gun."

Jim and Sally crouch down in the bushes and watch the man on the beach.

Suddenly Jim whispers, "Look, Sally. There's another boat out there on the sea."

Not far from the island they can both see the dark shape of a bigger boat in the moonlight. It has no lights.

"It looks like a motor yacht," whispers Jim. "It must be the smugglers' boat. One of the rowingboats must belong to them – and the other must belong to Mr. Carstairs from Sandy Bay. Now I understand."

"But what can we do, if that man is guarding the boats?"

"Wait a moment," says Jim. "I have an idea." He picks up a stone.

"Watch."

Jim throws the stone. It lands on the beach about twenty yards from the man.

The man looks up. He drops his cigarette on the beach and puts his foot on it.

Jim throws another stone. It lands in the same place.

The man stands up. They hear his voice. "Who's there?"

Jim throws another stone.

The man begins to walk across the beach away from the boats. Now he is ten yards from the boats – now he is nearly twenty yards … "Who's there?" says the man again.

1 **to guard** [ɡɑːd] bewachen 4 **gun** [ɡʌn] Gewehr 5 **to watch** [wɒtʃ] beobachten 10 **bigger** [ˈbɪɡə] größer 14 **to belong to** [bɪˈlɒŋ] gehören 19 **stone** [stəʊn] Stein 21 **to throw** [θrəʊ] werfen 22 **yard** [jɑːd] Yard, ca. 0,9 m 23 **to look up** aufschauen 23 **to drop** [drɒp] fallen lassen 25 **the same** [seɪm] der-, die-, dasselbe 27 **to stand up** aufstehen

"Now!" says Jim suddenly. "Into the nearest boat, Sally. Come on!"

Jim and Sally race down the beach to the nearest boat. Sally jumps in, Jim pushes the boat out, jumps in, and begins to row.

The man is running back along the beach. They hear his voice.

"Hey! Stop! Come back!"

"Faster! Faster!" says Sally. "He's getting into the other boat. He's following us."

Jim can see the man. He is pushing the other boat into the water. Jim rows with all his strength.

"Faster! Faster!" says Sally again. "He mustn't catch us."

1 **the nearest** ['nɪərəst] der, die, das nächste (der Entfernung nach) 8 **Hey!** [heɪ] He! / Heda! 9 **faster** ['fɑːstə] schneller 12 **strength** [streŋθ] Kraft 13 **he mustn't = he must not** [mʌsnt] er darf nicht

The Coastguards are Coming

The coastguard cutter is speeding towards the island. The searchlight is shining straight ahead. Suddenly the coastguard officer shouts, “Rowing boat ahead!”

“Where?” Mr. Baker is looking over the officer’s shoulder.

“A boy and a girl in the boat,” says the officer. “I can see them clearly. The boy is rowing.”

“It’s Jim and Sally!” shouts Mr. Baker.

“There’s another boat just behind them,” says the officer.

“Hurry! Hurry!” says Mr. Baker.

Soon they reach the first boat. Jim and Sally climb into the cutter.

“Jim! Sally!” Mr. Baker is overjoyed to see them.

“Dad!” Sally throws herself into Mr. Baker’s arms.

For a moment they forget about the man in the other boat.

Then Jim says, “Quick! We must catch that man in the other boat. He’s a smuggler. And there are four other smugglers on the island. One of them is Mr. Carstairs.”

“Smugglers?” Mr. Baker laughs. “Mr. Carstairs? What nonsense. You’re dreaming, Jim.”

“One moment,” says the coastguard officer. His face is very serious. “What do you know about Mr. Carstairs, Jim?”

Jim quickly tells the officer about the men in the hut. “There’s a motor yacht out there, too,” he says.

2 **straight** [streit] gerade 2 **ahead** [ə'hed] voraus, vorwärts 2 **straight ahead** geradeaus 13 **to climb** [klaɪm] klettern 15 **to be overjoyed** [əʊvə'dʒɔɪd] entzückt (*hier:* außer sich vor Freude) sein 16 **herself** [həself] sich 24 **to dream** [driːm] träumen 29 **out there** da draußen

"That's the smugglers' boat, I'm sure. But catch that man in the other rowing boat. He's one of them."

"Right, Jim," says the coastguard officer.

The motor roars. The man in the other boat is rowing back to the island, but they catch him before he reaches the beach.

In the hut on the island Mr. Carstairs is just counting the last gold watches.

"Right," he says to the smugglers. "£200,000 is my price. You can have the money from my bank in London the day after tomorrow, as always."

"Thank you, Mr. Carstairs," says one of the smugglers.

"And now we must take the boxes down to my boat," says Mr. Carstairs.

9 **£ = pound** [paʊnd] Pfund 10 **price** [praɪs] Preis, *hier:* Angebot 10 **bank** [bænk] Bank(haus) 11 **London** ['lʌndən] London 11 **the day after tomorrow** [tə'mɒrəʊ] übermorgen 11 **as always** [æz 'ɔːlweɪz] wie immer 14 **to take down** ['teɪk 'daʊn] *hier:* hinunter tragen

At that moment a light suddenly shines straight into their faces, and a voice from the door says, “Good evening, gentlemen.”

“What?! Who. …?” The smugglers stare at the light, dumb with astonishment.

“Stay where you are and don’t move,” says the coastguard officer sharply. “Good evening, Mr. Carstairs. There are a lot of questions that we want to ask you. I must ask all of you to come with me, please. There’s plenty of room on the coastguard cutter.”

The next morning breakfast is rather late in the Bakers’ holiday bungalow. It is eleven o’clock.

“Well, all’s well that ends well,” says Mr. Baker. “You helped the coastguards to catch a very big gang of

4 **to stare at** ['steər ə't] anstarren, hineinstarren 5 **dumb (with)** [dʌm] sprachlos (vor) 7 **sharply** *(adv.)* ['ʃɑːpli] scharf 10 **plenty of** ['plenti əv] eine Menge, reichlich 14 **all's well that ends well** ['ɔːls wel ðət 'endz wel] Ende gut, alles gut 15 **you helped** ['helpt] ihr halft / habt geholfen 15 **gang** [gæŋ] Bande

smugglers, so I mustn't punish you. But we were very worried – especially your mother."

"I'm very sorry, Dad," says Jim.

"All right," says Mr. Baker. "But don't go out so far again in old Martin's boat."

"No, Dad," says Jim.

"Promise?" says Mr. Baker.

"Promise," says Jim.

1 **to punish** ['pʌnɪʃ] (be)strafen 1 **we were** [wi wɜː] wir waren 2 **especially** [ɪs'peʃəli] besonders 7 **Promise?** ['prɒmɪs] Versprichst du's? / Versprecht ihr's?

Activities

1. **Questions on the text:**
Answer the questions. Write full sentences.

a) How old are Jim and Sally?

Jim is ____________ *and Sally is* ____________ .

b) Why are Jim and Sally Baker at Sandy Bay?

____ .

c) Who is Martin?

____ .

d) What do Jim and Sally discover near the middle of the island?

____ .

e) Why is the rowing boat gone when Jim and Sally reach the beach?

____ .

f) Why are Mr. Baker and old Martin at the police station?

____ .

g) Why does Jim wake up during the night?

____ .

h) Who is Mr. Carstairs?

______________________________________ .

i) How do Jim and Sally escape?

______________________________________ .

j) Why mustn't Mr. Baker punish Jim and Sally.

______________________________________ .

2. Match the following words:
Combine one of the words on the left with one of the words on the right.

rowing	station	______________
motor	ahead	______________
holiday	speed	______________
coastguard	tide	______________
full	bungalow	______________
straight	boat	______________
high	yacht	______________

3. Crossword puzzle: Put in the missing words. Find the words in the grey boxes.

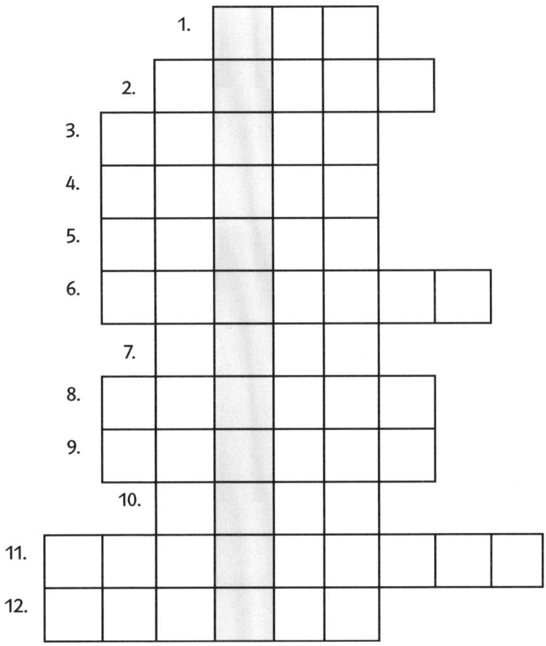

1. The coastguard cutter speeds across the dark … .
2. There are two rowing boats on the … .
3. At Sandy Bay there are … and cliffs and a beach.
4. One of the smugglers is shining a … into the box.
5. The island is covered with bushes and … .
6 The box is full of gold …, rings, and necklaces.
7. The boat drifted away with the … .
8. It is not easy to find a way through the … .
9. Jim says, "Let's go … ."
10. The boat is in order and the … are still in it.
11. Jim can see the four men clearly in the … .
12. The moon is shining through the … .

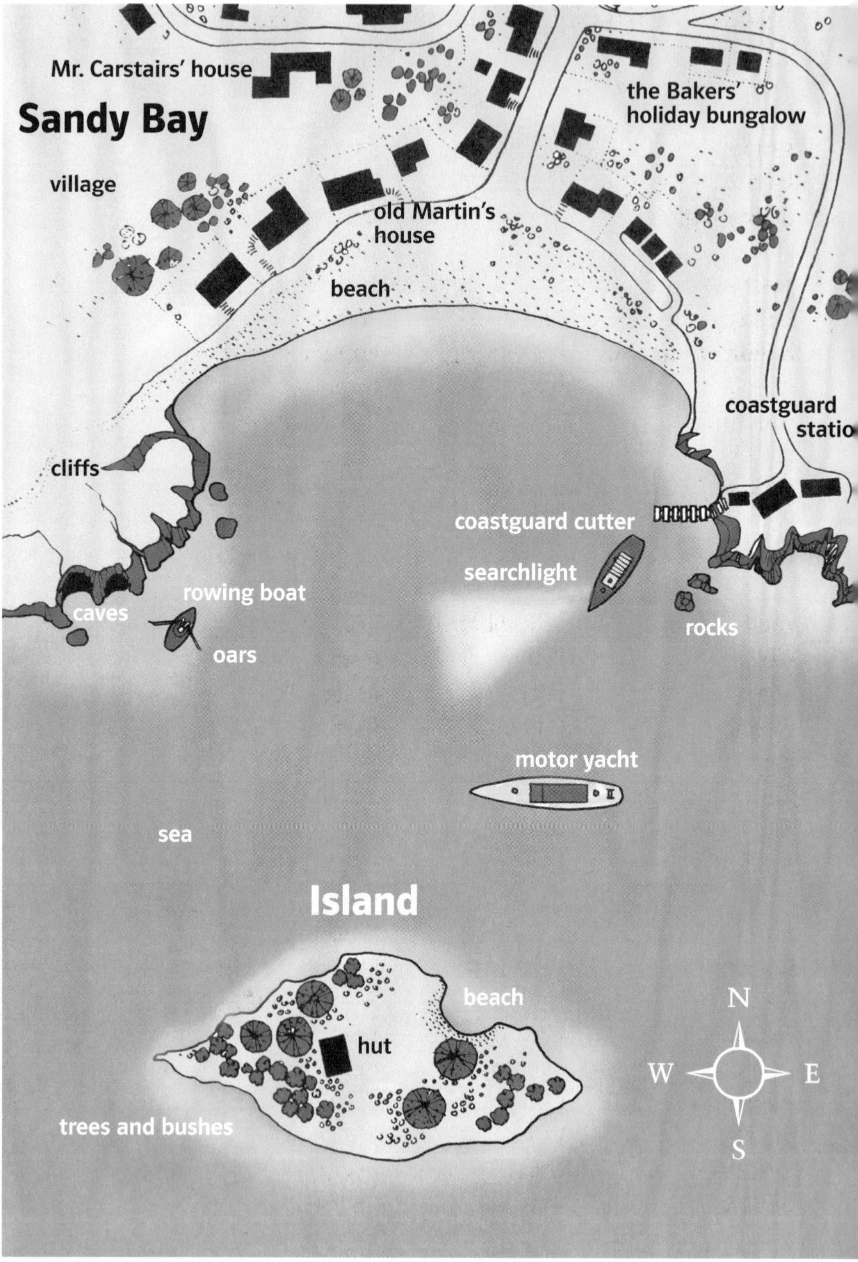
Mr. Carstairs' house
Sandy Bay
village
old Martin's house
the Bakers' holiday bungalow
beach
coastguard statio
cliffs
coastguard cutter
searchlight
rowing boat
caves
oars
rocks
motor yacht
sea
Island
beach
hut
N
W
E
S
trees and bushes

Map of Sandy Bay

sandy	['sændi]	sandig
bay	[beɪ]	Bucht
Sandy Bay		Ortsname
village	['vɪlɪʒ]	Dorf
police station	[pə'liːs 'steɪʃən]	Polizeiwache
holiday	['hɒlədeɪ]	Ferien
holiday bungalow	['bʌŋgələʊ]	Ferienwohnung
beach	[biːtʃ]	Strand
coastguard	['kəʊstgɑːd]	Küstenwache
cutter	['kʌtə]	Kutter
searchlight	['sɜːtʃlaɪt]	Scheinwerfer
cliff	[klɪf]	Klippe
cave	[keɪv]	Höhle
rock	[rɒk]	Felsen
rowing boat	['rəʊɪŋbəʊt]	Ruderboot
oar	[ɔː]	Ruder
sea	[siː]	Meer
motor	['məʊtə]	Motor
yacht	[jɒt]	Jacht
tree	[triː]	Baum
bush	[bʊʃ]	Busch
hut	[hʌt]	Hütte
island	['aɪlənd]	Insel
mile	[maɪl]	Meile, etwa 1,5 km
Carstairs	['kɑːsteəz]	Familienname
Baker	['beɪkə]	Familienname
Martin	['mɑːtin]	Martin
secret	['siːkrɪt]	Geheimnis
missing	['mɪsɪŋ]	vermisst
night	[naɪt]	Nacht
search	[sɜːtʃ]	Suche
escape	[ɪs'keɪp]	Flucht

Solutions

1. Questions on the text
a) Jim is thirteen and Sally is twelve.
b) Jim and Sally are at Sandy Bay because they are on holiday with their parents.
c) Martin is an old fisherman.
d) They discover a small hut.
e) The boat is gone because it drifted away with the tide.
f) They are at the police station because Jim and Sally are missing.
g) Jim wakes up because four smugglers are coming towards the hut.
h) Mr. Carstairs is a smuggler.
i) They take one of the smugglers' rowing boats.
j) He mustn't punish Jim and Sally because they helped the coastguards to catch a very big gang of smugglers.

2. Match the following words
rowing boat, motor yacht, holiday bungalow, coastguard station, full speed, straight ahead, high tide

3. Crossword puzzle

			1.	s	e	a			
		2.	b	e	a	c	h		
	3.	r	o	c	k	s			
	4.	t	o	r	c	h			
	5.	t	r	e	e	s			
	6.	w	a	t	c	h	e	s	
		7.	t	i	d	e			
	8.	b	u	s	h	e	s		
	9.	i	n	l	a	n	d		
		10.	o	a	r	s			
11.	m	o	o	n	l	i	g	h	t
12.	w	i	n	d	o	w			

Note:
secret island – geheime Insel
the secret of the island – das Geheimnis der Insel